SOCIAL MEDIA VS. SOCIAL LEARNING

The emergence and popularity of social tools has brought with it a good deal of confusion over terms. Social learning is not new: It's how we've always learned. We talk, we watch others, and we tell and show each other how to do things. We learn our native languages not from formal instruction but by moving in our environments, listening, and practicing with others. Social media is a tool that can support social learning on a bigger scale: across geography, time, and organizational boundaries. This *Infoline* offers an explanation of ways social media tools can be used to support social learning efforts in both formal and informal ways.

This *Infoline* will show you how to:

- separate myth from fact in approaching the use of social media tools for learning

- replicate parts of existing training and development (T&D) practice using social tools

- extend current practice through the use of social tools

- support change in moving to use of social tools for workplace learning.

MYTHBUSTING

Let's take a look first at some popular myths about social media, particularly in regards to the public sector. Most are more misunderstandings or generalizations than insurmountable barriers.

Myth #1: Government Can't Use Social Media

It's a popular myth that some industries "can't" use social media: healthcare, regulatory banking, and government are commonly referenced. But in reality, it just isn't so. The Mayo Clinic is an exemplar of social media use in healthcare, providing everything from Twitter chats for patients, to video profiles of doctors, to training for staff in choosing tools and creating nimble content. SunTrust Bank utilizes

MARINES ON FACEBOOK

The U.S. Marine Corps recognizes that social media tools can play a vital role in connecting soldiers to their communities and families. Additionally, according to the Marine Corp's website, "Marines are encouraged to responsibly engage in unofficial Internet posts about the Marine Corps and Marine Corps-related topics. The Marine Corps performs a valuable service around the world every day and Marines are often in the best position to share the Marine Corps' story with the domestic and foreign publics." While there's no public surfacing of using social media explicitly for learning among the troops, the effort here contradicts the myth that government "can't" use social media.

There are guidelines for posting, but they aren't too onerous or lengthy. For the most part, they offer guidance about integrity, and recognition that online comments are permanent, the opinions of the person posting, and the responsibility of the one posting. There's also advice about privacy settings and computer security useful for everyone.

For more information visit: www.marines.mil/News/SocialMedia/Guidance.aspx.

a variety of social media-based approaches for strengthening ties with customers. In government there is perhaps no better example of social media use than that provided by the U.S. Department of Defense (DoD). Internal communication and learning, as well as increased public interest and the expectation of transparency driven by the Open Government Initiative, have led the DoD to many initiatives utilizing social media. Activities span both in-house and external efforts (such as outreach to veterans) as well as implicit support for employee use of social media, such as guidelines offered to U.S. Marines wishing to use social media tools. For more about the Marines' social media guidelines read, *Marines on Facebook* above.

Why is it that one state government can not only allow, but actively encourage, employee social media use, while a neighboring state restricts everything? Why can one hospital brand itself as a leader in using social media to strengthen bonds with patients, while a competitor refuses to engage in any social media

CONNECTING AGENCIES TO THE PUBLIC

Below are some examples of government organizations that are using social media tools to connect with the public.

State Department State Department CO.NX

The U.S. Department of State includes CO.NX, a diplomacy team with the Bureau of International Information Programs. The agency's "digital diplomacy" initiative connects people around the world with State Department officials and others using live interactive web chats, live Q&A sessions, and video chats. According to their website, the mission "is to help create connections between people and provide a virtual space for the interactive exchange of ideas." CO.NX is explicitly working to encourage contact, create content, and support connectivity. In other words, CO.NX has created a space that encourages and fosters social and informal learning. The agency employs multiple platforms, including a custom portal, as well as YouTube, Twitter, and iTunes, and supports conversations in multiple languages. Upcoming events include chats on drug abuse prevention, cancer, and Internet freedom. See https://conx.state.gov/.

Real Warriors Campaign

The Real Warriors Campaign, overseen by the Defense Centers of Excellence for Psychological Health and Traumatic Brain Injury (DCoE), is part of the Department of Defense's initiative to provide support for those dealing with post-traumatic stress disorder and other combat-related problems. The multifaceted effort combines formal education programs, phone support, and social media tools (Facebook, Twitter, YouTube, and live chats) in an effort to connect with and help service members, veterans, and military families. See www.realwarriors.net/aboutus.

activities at all? Mostly it's culture. Having someone at (or near) the top who sees value more than threat and who clears obstacles such as IT restrictions and questions about productivity, seems to matter more than anything else. Finding and clearing bottlenecks and resistance in the middle is often a challenge. One large federal agency issued a directive that frontline workers can begin using social media to engage with the public, only to find later that IT managers at the local level were failing to implement and support the directive. That's a management problem, not a technology problem. For examples of government agencies who have had success, see *Connecting Agencies to the Public*.

Myth #2: Social Media Is Free

The public tools are free, true. But planning to use them to support a community, conduct training-related activities, and extend existing practice is not. There is a commitment of someone's time and energy to learn the tool, make meaningful connections, engage in worthwhile conversation, build a personal learning network, nurture the community, respond to comments, and find or develop fresh content. There will be time spent on planning and—depending upon choices made—there may be time needed to iron out concerns with IT and legal, and train users to use tools. Using proprietary or internal tools may bring additional costs. Going in with a realistic view of the resources needed will help make your efforts more successful.

Myth #3: If You Build It, They Will Come

The critical element of social media is that it is social. Government entities wishing to use it to support workplace learning will need to identify ways of engaging with learners and participating in conversations, not just pushing content; an additional requirement is to have people who are willing to do this. Too frequently a trainer says something like, "I created an online group but they won't post to it." While there are plenty of tools and ways of publishing information and pushing content, optimal use of social media will require approaches that encourage inclusion and participation from all parties involved.

Battling the Myths

New technologies and approaches always bring with them a swirl of rumor, conjecture, excitement, fear, and yes, hype. The practitioner wishing to use social tools should choose two or three that she finds especially appealing and work to become proficient with those. In this way, you can learn firsthand where myth meets reality, and can be better positioned to have informed conversations with stakeholders about goals and implementation plans.

STRATEGY MATTERS

Before embarking on an effort to incorporate social media into training practice, it's critical to identify the problem you're trying to solve. "We need to do social media" or "we need to start an online group" is not a strategy. What exactly are you hoping to accomplish? Here are some examples of objectives that could be accomplished through a social media strategy:

- Address a particular performance problem.
- Cultivate relationships with your learner base or outside customers.
- Support department branding or increase presence.
- Connect pools of talent or expertise.
- Host a training course.
- Support the alumni of a course.
- Facilitate communities of employees (or customers) with particular talents or interests.
- Expand the reach of the training department.
- Support learner engagement post-training event.

Working With Tools to Support Your Strategy

As with any other tool, the effectiveness—or lack thereof—is more about how the tool is used rather than the tool itself: The hammer is not responsible for the quality of the house. The intrinsic benefit of new social tools is their capacity for helping people connect, share, and interact. While you can use them to deliver information and broadcast assignments, doing so is not really employing them for the things they can uniquely support. Co-creation and collaboration are the currencies of the new digital work: Try to get beyond simple publication and call-and-response activities to endeavors that encourage learner participation, self-direction, and interaction.

That being said, it's important to know what kinds of tools are out there and how they can best be leveraged for your social media efforts. Social media tools today tend to fall into several distinct "buckets." There are picture-sharing tools, such as Pinterest and Flickr; publishing tools, such as blogs; collaboration tools like wikis or Google Docs; shared bookmarking tools, for example, Diigo and Delicious; microblogging tools like Twitter and Yammer; social profile tools, such as LinkedIn; and aggregators— tools that do a bit of everything—like Facebook. Video tools such as YouTube and Vimeo have become popular for quick tutorials on everything from music to auto repair. Google Hangouts is an easy tool for video chats that can be recorded and uploaded to YouTube. Many organizations are using Microsoft Sharepoint, a suite of products for document management, sharing, and conversation. Google Apps likewise offers a suite of products, from email to collaborative tools like shared calendars and documents, which are available as the Google Apps for Government suite that is now in use by more than 40 government agencies.

It's important to understand that most tools can be used for most things. All the tools can, for instance, publish or broadcast information. You can deliver a newsletter with a blogging tool, or use it to host a discussion. You could run a book club on Twitter, LinkedIn, on a blog, or most anywhere else different people can post comments. You can publish photos to Pinterest or to Facebook. Or you may have the need to use proprietary or in-house tools. It's not so much a matter of choosing "the one" right tool as the one that works best for your situation. Think about learning goals and strategy.

The Choosing Tools job aid at the end of this *Infoline* provides a quick overview of types of tools popular now. There is—at least at this time—no one perfect tool, nor is there a simple answer to "which tools should I pick?" This depends largely on your strategy (do you want to broadcast information or nurture a learning community?) as well as what your organization will allow and learners will use. Be careful of "toolitis": It's tempting to want to try a bit of everything, but this can create confusion for learners. Start out with one or two tools that support your goals and adjust or add on later.

ASSESSING VALUE

The age of analytics and Big Data has brought with it the expectation that all activities will bring some sort of tangible return. Unfortunately, with social connections and interactions (regardless of whether tools are used or not) there is just no magic algorithm that will pull quantifiable meaning from conversation and observation. This is further complicated by the fact that for many of us, the line between work and play is increasingly blurry: a casual contact made while participating in an online conversation about a hobby may turn out to be someone with valuable work-related information to share. Etienne Wenger, well-known for his work with social learning and apprenticeship, offers this new framework for assessing value in online interactions. The framework asks that we look across a span, starting with reasons for engagement and development of social connections, then asks whether the worker is making use of those connections in ways that benefit him or the organization. One trick: surfacing that information in useful ways, an issue discussed at great length by the framework authors.

FIGURE 1.1: Value Creation in Communities and Networks

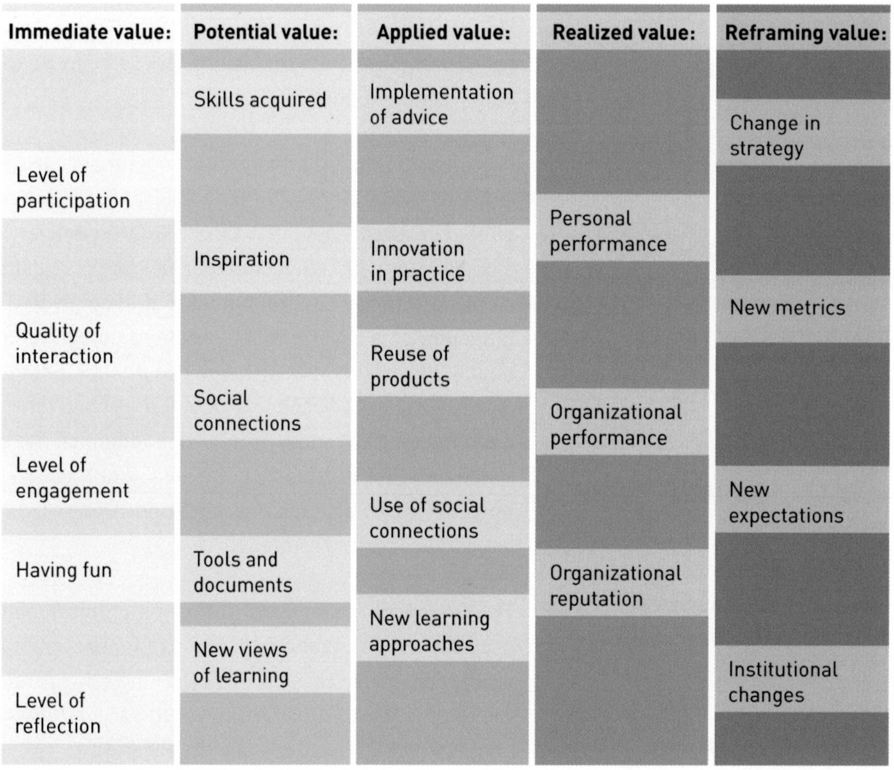

Immediate value:	Potential value:	Applied value:	Realized value:	Reframing value:
	Skills acquired	Implementation of advice		Change in strategy
Level of participation			Personal performance	
	Inspiration	Innovation in practice		New metrics
Quality of interaction		Reuse of products		
	Social connections		Organizational performance	
Level of engagement		Use of social connections		New expectations
Having fun	Tools and documents		Organizational reputation	
	New views of learning	New learning approaches		Institutional changes
Level of reflection				

The framework is pulled from a long whitepaper available at: http://wenger-trayner.com/resources/publications/evaluation-framework/ and is used with permission.

Most heavy users of social media for work will tell you that one of the greatest benefits comes from developing a Personal Learning Network (PLN): contacts who share information of value to you, who participate in the community, and who respond and ask for help. The PLN grows from interactions, observations, and development of connections, and is dependent on the efforts of the individual seeking to grow one.

Public vs. Private and External vs. Internal

Tools can be implemented in either public or private ways (for example, a public Facebook group versus a secret one); or through means that are either entirely external (Facebook) or internal (such as Sharepoint, Jive, Yammer, and other tools available inside organization firewalls). There are often good reasons for wanting to keep conversations private, such as those that might include sharing of proprietary information. And in truth, taxpayers have the right to—and do—scrutinize the ways in which government employees spend time; it's important not to look as if workers are hanging around on social sites all day. But some conversations can gain value from being shared with the world outside the organization, and some processes can be improved by inviting the opinions of others. Think of conversations about improved hiring practices, how other agencies or whole governments motivate staff, issues related to customer service, or book chats about leadership practices. If private in-house conversation is critical, then by all means use tools for that. But don't overlook opportunities to encourage connection with expertise and information outside the walls of your own organization. Provide guidelines if necessary—and remember, if you have communication policies in place, you likely already have those guidelines covered.

REPLICATING PRACTICE USING NEW TOOLS

The T&D practitioner will find that social tools can lend themselves easily to replicating existing practice. Traditional activities such as icebreakers and group discussions can be supported—and perhaps enhanced—with new tools. This may be an excellent way of dipping a toe into new technology waters, as practitioners can use their existing facilitation and activity-guiding skills in new settings. Once you're comfortable with the tools though, try to move past just publishing or broadcasting information and assignments. The real magic is in the ways they can help learners connect and learn from and with one another. A change for T&D is in the growing need to participate as well as push

content. It's important for practitioners to become members and partners in the learning process, not bystanders, supervisors, or "facilitators." This nurtures community, extends your reach, and creates a tighter relationship between learning and performance.

Before Class

An easy entry to using social media for workplace learning is as a means of distributing prework and assignments. Social media tools can be a great way to broadcast course information including logistics, agendas, objectives, and outlines, and materials such as readings or videos. This can help participants get an overview of the course and clarify goals and desired outcomes.

Introductions and Icebreakers

Also before class, participants can offer introductions quickly using microblogging tools or an online group, blog, or profile site. Replicating practice is quite easy here, whether it is asking participants to offer some brief autobiographical information (job title, work area) and goals regarding the training at hand (for example, one thing they already know, one thing they'd like to know, one thing they hope to take away, greatest challenge with the topic, reason for enrolling, and so on). People who will be together for an extended program might be encouraged to offer something a bit more personal, such as a favorite hobby, sports team, or other interest.

Many popular training icebreakers can be easily replicated using social tools. For instance, the familiar "reach into your pocket and choose an item that represents you, then explain why" is easily repurposed to most social tools by replacing "item" with a picture, quote, book title, or movie character. Most icebreaker-type activities involve some sort of personal disclosure, sharing goals or experiences, or practice in learning names or interests. Consider your own favorites and cull them down to their essence: Do they ask people to offer three statements that others then comment on? Do they share images or draw an idea? A new technology-mediated favorite: Ask participants to post a photo of their cube, office, or other workspace.

Games

It's easy to set up a first-answer, round robin, or scavenger-hunt type game using most social media tools. Take a look at games you're using now and consider ways they could be replicated. Timed games, for instance, work very well on microblogging tools, where answers will pop up more quickly and are more easily viewed than as comments on a blog. A photo-based scavenger hunt can be hosted on most any tool that allows for photo uploads, especially in a Flickr group or on a shared Pinterest board.

Watch and Respond Video

The interface for popular public video sites most often offers space for the video itself with an area nearby for comments. The possibilities here should be evident: Distribute a clip and ask for learner response. For instance, a video showing a difficult interaction during a performance review might prompt you to ask learners: "What should the supervisor say next?" or "What did the supervisor do well?" "What might he have done instead?" or "How is the employee likely to respond?"

There are a number of options here: YouTube, Vimeo, and TeacherTube are a few popular public video products. Some organizations have their own internal video channels. Many people don't realize that YouTube offers private channels—so videos and the comment space are visible only to selected people—and allows learners to subscribe to channels. They receive an alert whenever a new video is posted. Consider the possibilities for offering bi-weekly course follow-up 'reminder' videos or bimonthly videos on a topic area like leadership, safety, or workplace-specific skills.

In thinking about the use of video, don't overlook opportunities here for user-generated content. A quick clip showing how the repairman fixed the part, how the administrative assistant sets up the equipment, or a worker talking through how she arrived at a particular decision, helps include learners, shares tacit knowledge, and expands the reach of the T&D function.

Intersession Work

Social media tools can help to fill the gaps between formal training sessions. Intersession work can spur reflection, help connect one session to the next, and help new ideas keep a place in learners' minds. Try sharing links to readings and slides, and short videos, including some starring you or other instructors. You can post a reading and ask for reflection, post a video and ask for reactions, or post a slideshow and ask for ideas for applying new information. Use social media to ask participants how they have applied key content. For example: "Tuesday we covered the benefits of using empathy in corrective conversations. Where have you had the opportunity to employ empathy with staff this week?" It's a given for most of us in the field that the most interesting questions get asked just as class time ends. Use social tools to continue these conversations.

Use this opportunity to set the stage for upcoming learning by posting information about next week's topic and asking for reactions or suggesting that learners become mindful about a skill they'll be working on. For example: "Next week we'll be talking about motivations and recognition. What has made you feel energized and motivated this week? Where do you see your staff showing unusual interest or energy?"

Group Work

Collaboration tools—those that people can share, particularly in real time—can make co-creation a much more efficient and interesting process. Tools like wikis and Google Docs allow everyone to work on something together: a definition, a new process, improving an existing process, a new work tool, a group newsletter on "what my work unit is doing," or documentation of a group project. Or you can create a space, such as a wiki, where leaders and mentors can share expertise on retaining talent, streamlining work, or managing their own stress. Looking for an easy use for collaborative documents? Ask anyone taking notes in your class to use a shared document (and take turns if they like). This will let everyone have a course book to access later and give you an interesting means of formative evaluation. Such books created over time can also give you documentation of iterations course.

Discussions

A subset of "discussion" options with social media is the easy way of bringing in an expert. This could be anyone in the company, an outside expert, an author, or well-known presenter. Many are amenable for a quick chat, and most tools lend themselves easily to text chatting or, with tools like Google Hangouts, video chats. These tools offer the opportunity for debates, conversations, or meet the expert sessions.

Start discussions on different content areas (for instance, empathy, teamwork, and motivation) and ask learners to add to these throughout the course. Set up a debate or role play on something from the course content. Appoint weekly "experts" to become especially fluent in content covered in that time, and support them in teaching it to or answering questions from others. Invite discussions about critical incidents: a time the performance review went badly, a workplace accident occurred, a system failure took place, or when a surprisingly stunning success evolved.

Photos can serve as especially good ways to spark a discussion. Just asking, "What's wrong with this picture?" or "What should the worker do differently?" can be enough to generate interest and comments.

FAQs

Set up a page, or pages, and ask learners to work together to build a list of frequently asked questions (FAQs) about topic areas. This can be set as an assignment on a time limit or continue through the course. This can be a takeaway for learners in a particular course, or kept as an evolving tool for all learners over multiple sessions of the same course.

Class Notes

Wikis can help learners develop a permanent, searchable record of notes from live class sessions. Start a new wiki page for every class session and have learners create and edit notes as they go. Different learners can enter data in different fonts, colors, or sign off with initials—or simply add anonymously to the ongoing list.

EVALUATING CREDIBILITY OF "EXPERTS"

Organizations frequently turn to subject matter experts for help understanding new approaches, and social media is no exception. In evaluating the credibility of consultants and trainers look for things that indicate they are not only using, but engaging with, the tools. They don't necessarily need to be active in every social channel but should use a variety and be able to articulate why they chose each. Pay attention to their overall activity and the ways that they interact.

Hosting Courses

It's possible to use social tools for hosting an entire course. More robust tools like Facebook or LinkedIn, or an online group site such as Google Groups or Ning, can support the array of needs a course instructor might have: introductions, pre-class work, activities, posting assignments and readings, hosting discussions, and providing follow-up conversations and information.

Evaluation

Social tools are excellent for garnering evaluative feedback. For summative evaluation, at the end of a session ask learners to share one key takeaway, one actionable idea, or one plan for how they will implement a concept. Schedule posts (you can do this with most tools, including blogs, Twitter, and Facebook) 14, 30, and 60 days out asking what actions participants have taken and what results they achieved. Also ask for feedback about the course itself: Which activities were memorable? What information seemed to "stick" best? For summative feedback during sessions, or in between, ask people to share a key point, from the morning or previous day. This will help you gauge whether learners are "getting it" while you have time to adjust your plan if need be.

TIPS FOR GROWING A COMMUNITY

1. **Know the audience and their needs.** Often what learners want to talk about seems to be at odds with what T&D is talking about. New hires don't care about endless policies and rules; they want to know how to get approved for tuition reimbursement programs, strategies for getting on board and getting ahead, and the 'real' process for getting office supplies.

2. **Appreciate.** "Thank you" goes a long way. So does "Welcome, let me introduce you to _____."

3. **Pay attention.** Who comments frequently, writes longer comments, or is especially passionate or articulate? Invite them in as guest authors or co-administrators. Highlight contributions.

4. **Have reasonable expectations.** As with any other endeavor, it's not reasonable to expect 100 percent participation from 100 percent of a target audience. Recognize that there will always be nonparticipants, quieter voices, and those who simply are not interested. Work to strengthen ties with more engaged participants.

5. **Step back.** Try not to be the only voice talking. Try to be a participant in the conversation, not the sole leader.

6. **Be patient.** As with a garden, it's usual for time to elapse between planting and seeing results.

Sustaining Learning

Many of the ideas offered for intersession work will work here as well, including just occasionally reminding learners "we covered this, how have you used that?" or posting a link to a related article. The tools can be used for coaching, for addressing any follow-up issues, and for staying in touch with learners by asking how they're doing.

SUPPORTING SUCCESS

While this *Infoline* isn't intended to serve as a guide to change management, it would be unrealistic to suggest that the use of new technologies and approaches can happen without creating some disruptions in a system. There are several things you can do to get support for new initiatives:

- **Understand threats.** You will have more productive conversations if you understand the point of view of the other person or entity. The IT department may have concerns about security, management may be worried about productivity, and legal may warn about confidentiality. Work to address these rather than fight them by showing real examples and cases of other organizations successfully using tools. Provide examples of simple, common-sense use guidelines such as those from the Mayo Clinic or Ford Motor Company, offer employee training in acceptable behaviors and content that can or cannot be shared, and focus on small pilots rather than enterprise-wide endeavors. Build on small successes.

- **State your case.** "We need to do social media" or "I must have a Facebook page" is not a strategy, and they aren't likely to get you much support. Try: "We have a lot of knowledge being lost in the field and I need to find a way to help us capture that. I need something that will let the techs talk as well as upload pictures and videos of their solutions." Or, "I need a tool that will let graduates of our leadership academy stay connected after the course ends. The old online forums are too clunky."

- **Leverage what's already there.** The odds are good that your agency already has some social media activity in place, in your public information office or your marketing department. Work with them to better understand obstacles or possible problems and address these early on. If possible, partner with these areas and add on to what they are already doing rather than expend all your energy creating stand-alone initiatives.

MOVING FORWARD

A challenge for the T&D practitioner is staying current. New tools emerge, old tools are bought and absorbed by others, and some disappear altogether. One trend on the horizon is that of the user-generated image. With cell phones nearly ubiquitous among U.S. workers—most with cameras—the ease and comfort level of working with digital photography is changing internet behavior. They are moving past web surfing and consuming content to sharing. Pew Internet Research reports that as of 2012, 47 percent—nearly half—of adults online are uploading and sharing images. This speaks to quick and easy knowledge capture—a picture of how the hedges should be trimmed, a photo of inserting the custom shim to steady the paper tray, or snapshots of the whiteboard notes uploaded to the work group. It also invites participation from some who may have been marginalized by the text-heavy tools of the past, such as low-literacy workers, those whose primary language differs from that of the bulk of the workforce, or people who are just not strong writers.

Government has recognized the potential for online images. For instance, the Library of Congress is already leveraging the ability to publish photos online—the Flickr stream has frequent updates and allows for viewer comments, while the U.S. Army is active on Pinterest. See the references section for links.

SOCIAL MEDIA SKILLS AND NEW ROLES

New approaches also bring new skill sets and roles for the T&D practitioner. Several of these are discussed below.

Curator

"Information overload" is a growing problem. The T&D professional can serve a critical role in helping to filter information and get it in front of learners. Curating is more than aggregation, amassing of piles of material. Rather, the curator vets and assembles information around a particular topic, point of view, or accepted practice. But T&D needn't be the only workhorse for this: Recruit learners and others to help in your efforts.

Community Manager

In this role, manage a work group, you facilitate a course, and you nurture a community. Discussions on community management often call up gardening metaphors: nurturing, seeding, and even weeding are critical. Start conversations, offer readings and ask for a response, bring up an organizational happenings and ask for comment. Some tips:

1. Be sure the topic is something others want to discuss. Really, most people just aren't very interested in discussing things like the organization's bureaucratic policies. Find the "water cooler" conversations that already engage them. Museum community manager Julian Stodd says, "A primary reason people don't engage in social learning spaces is because the story is not relevant." Find the stories they care about to draw them in.

2. Realize you don't have to do it all yourself. Recruit some ambassadors or deputies who can help with posting new topics or participating in conversations. You can even feed content to them to post under their names so everything isn't coming from you. This can be especially useful when a community is new.

3. Have reasonable expectations. Every course graduate will not join your community (nor will every employee in the organization), and the ones that do will not participate equally. People will come and go. Recognize that a community is a breathing organism, not a fixed entity.

4. Have a plan, but don't over-manage. It's OK to have a few ground rules, but too many rules will squelch participation. Decide ahead of time how you will deal with inappropriate or acrimonious comments, chronic complainers, or people who break rules about things like profanity.

5. The arguments for anonymous comments go both ways: People who can post anonymously may tell 'truths' worth hearing, or feel more comfortable posting without feeling they are being scrutinized. On the other hand, requiring posters to use their real names does tend to cut down on the amount of inappropriate comments and angry fights.

6. A warning: Be careful of building too many silos. If there is already an active community on Facebook discussing "ethics in government practice" then your attempts to grow another one in another place may end up being a lot of effort with little payoff. There are literally dozens of online groups dedicated, one way or another, to "training and development." Most groups include many of the same people, the same conversations, and the same dynamics.

IS THAT OPPORTUNITY KNOCKING?

K-12 educators, dealing with children, have special challenges as government employees seeking to use new technologies. With so much conversation in the public space focused on using social media with children, Principal Joe Mazza focuses not on use with kids but in strengthening ties with parents. For example, after creating a live feed so that parents unable to attend live parent-teacher organizations meetings could participate, attendance went from an average of 13 to 43. Other efforts, some using Facebook and Twitter, help develop awareness for parents of day-to-day school activities, special projects and programs, and builds bridges between faculty and parents. Extending the reach of our efforts is always critical for T&D; consider the possibilities of closer ties with supervisors and contact with learners as co-partners in your efforts. For more information, follow @joe_mazza on Twitter.

Supporter as Narrator

Social media lends itself perfectly to narrating work. First-person narratives of "my problem and how I solved it," "my mistake and how I fixed it," or "here's how I did that" can be critical to capturing organizational knowledge and helping others learn. Narratives can be written and posted to a blog; recorded and posted to a video channel; or sketched, photographed, and uploaded to any one of a number of tools. T&D is ideally positioned to support these efforts at identifying performers and helping to capture the narration and make it available to the workforce.

An interesting approach to narrating work is offered by the U.K. Ministry of Justice. The Digital Services Division offers a lot of interaction with the public, but most important to our discussion is the extensive use of colloquial first-person blogging to describe details of projects, decisions, and processes.

OTHER TOOLS

Space here dictates that we focus more on established, popular types of tools. Your needs may call out for something else, which may be found as a separate stand-alone solution or something that can be linked to or even integrated into another. For instance, there are dozens of good, free online tools for collaborative mindmapping and brainstorming, tools for shared whiteboarding, and "sticky note" or collage-building activities. There are myriad tools for calendaring, scheduling across time zones, and project management. If you find yourself wishing you could perform some particular activity with social media, take a look around—odds are that you probably can.

REFERENCES & RESOURCES

Bozarth, J. (2010). *Social Media for Trainers*. San Francisco: Pfeiffer.

Brenner, J. (2013). "Pew Internet: Social Networking." Accessed at: http://pewinternet.org/Commentary/2012/March/Pew-Internet-Social-Networking-full-detail.aspx.

Herman, J. (2013). "Pinterest Brings Social Image Sharing to Government" HowTo.Gov. Accessed at: http://blog.howto.gov/2013/01/17/pinterest-brings-social-image-sharing-to-government/.

Kotter, J. (1996). *Leading Change*. Cambridge, MA: Harvard University Press.

Wenger, E., B. Trayner, and M. de Laat (2012). "Promoting and Assessing Value in Communities and Networks: A Conceptual Framework." Accessed at: http://wenger-trayner.com/resources/publications/evaluation-framework/.

Willyerd, K. (2012). "Social Tools Can Improve Onboarding" *Harvard Business Review*. Accessed at: http://blogs.hbr.org/cs/2012/12/social_tools_can_improve_e.html.

Websites:

Course scrapbook the graduates made from a recent government train-the-trainer course: http://beta.mural.ly/!/#/JaneBozarth/1342089561073.

Hootsuite White Paper "Social Media in Government: 5 Key Considerations": http://socialbusiness.hootsuite.com/whitepaper-social-media-in-government.html.

Library of Congress Flickr page: www.flickr.com/photos/library_of_congress/.

More information on Joe Mazza's school social media plan: www3.bucksiu.org/cms/lib3/PA09000729/Centricity/Domain/50/BCIU_Mazza_eFACE_1-9-13.pdf.

Online database of social media policies: http://socialmediagovernance.com/policies.php.

The U.K. Ministry of Justice Digital Services: http://blogs.justice.gov.uk/digital/.

Updates for *Social Media for Trainers*: www.facebook.com/SoMe4Trainers .

CHOOSING TOOLS

Tool	Examples	What?	Uses	Limits	Important to know?
Microblogging	Twitter Yammer SocialText	Tool for posting quick comments, usually to a group or to the public	Quick, often loosely-structured discussions; good for quick thinkers	Can be chaotic; reflective thinkers can struggle. Most tools have character limit	Structure questions so that they can be answered within space or character constraints
Blog	Blogger WordPress	Easy-edit webpage creation tool	Online journals, post-and-respond conversations, course support	Typically limited use for conversation; of all the social tools offers the highest level of privacy and most control	Can be difficult to keep in front of users; anecdotally, expectation is that blog is the most "formal" of the tools
Social Profiles	Facebook Google+ LinkedIn MySpace	Individual's interests, career, education, status updates, groups	Building connections and relationships; participating in communities; locating others with similar skills or interests	Learners may need help understanding limits of personal or professional connections, and using privacy settings	Most tools have different levels of groups (for instance, Facebook groups can be public, private, or secret); invest time in learning about these features and using privacy settings
Wiki	PB Works Seedwiki Google Docs	Shared documents	Tools for collaboration and co-creation; can be shared in real time	Limited use for conversation	Simplest form of wiki is shared doc such as Google Doc
Photo Sharing	Flickr Pinterest	Online library or aggregator for user-generated images	Documenting machine repairs, organizational culture issues; narrating work, great potential for low-literacy or workers with different languages	Effective searching depends on effective tagging	Easy to use; adult internet users comfortable with photo sharing

Explore group capability; users need to be in agreement on tags to use |
| Social Bookmarking | Diigo Delicious | Easy-access web-based library of selected links; can be shared with group or made public | Sharing online resources; curating resources around a work interest or topic area | As with photo sites, success rests largely with effective tagging | As with photo sharing, explore group capability; users need to be in agreement on tags to use |
| Video Sites | YouTube Vimeo | Web-based library of public and/or user-generated video | Distributing information; requesting learner response to situation or scenario; inviting learner-generated submissions; narrating work | | Explore potential for strategic or instructional use of comment feature.

Note: Google Hangouts offer real-time video chats |